Anonymus

**Household Furniture in Genteel Taste for the Year 1760**

Anonymus

**Household Furniture in Genteel Taste for the Year 1760**

ISBN/EAN: 9783742816290

Manufactured in Europe, USA, Canada, Australia, Japa

Cover: Foto ©Thomas Meinert / pixelio.de

Manufactured and distributed by brebook publishing software
(www.brebook.com)

Anonymus

**Household Furniture in Genteel Taste for the Year 1760**

# HOUSHOLD FURNITURE

### In Genteel Taste, for the Year 1760.

by

## a Society of

## Upholsterers, Cabinet-Makers, &c.

### CONTAINING

## Upwards of 180 Designs

## on 60 Copper Plates.

Consisting of China, Breakfast, Side-board,
Dressing, Toilet; Card, Writing, Claw, Library,
Slab, and Night-Tables, Chairs, Couches, French-
Stools, Cabinets, Commodes, China Shelves and
Cases, Trays, Chests, Stands for Candles, Tea Kettles,
Pedestals, Stair-case Lights, Bureaus, Beds,
Ornamental Bed-posts, Cornuches, Brackets,
Fire Screens, Desk, Book and Clock-cases,
Frames for Glasses, Sconce & Chimney-pieces,
Girandoles, Lanthorns, Chandalears, &c. &c.

### with Scales.

London Printed for Rob.t Sayer, Map & Printseller,
at the Golden Buck, in Fleet Street.
Price 6.s Sewed, Bound 7.s 6.d

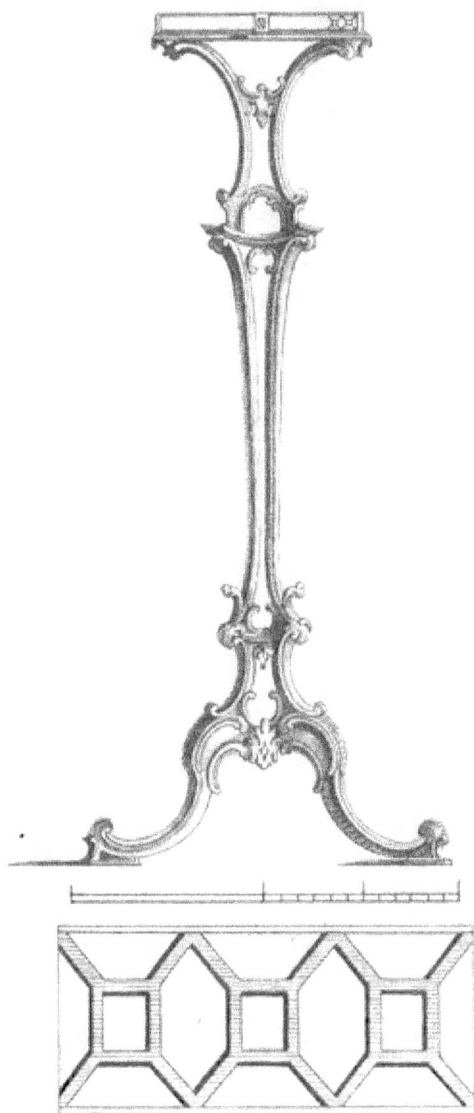

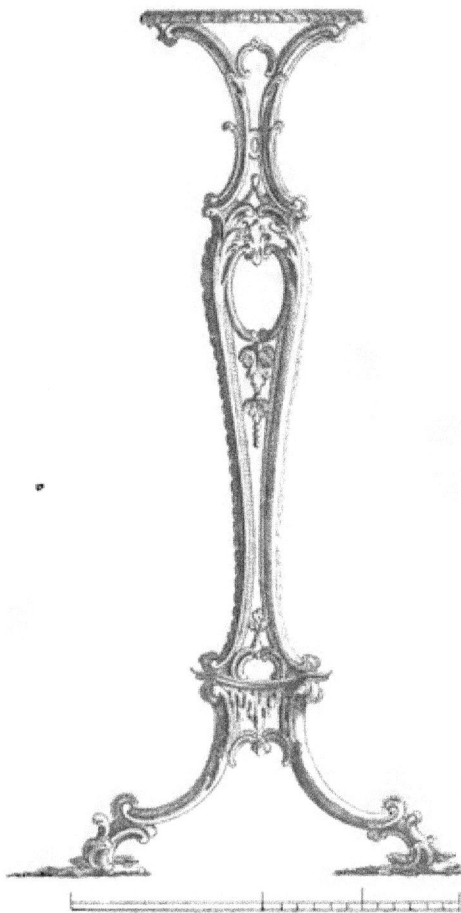

# Chandalier.

4

*Hall* *Lanthorn* ?

Stair-Case Lights.

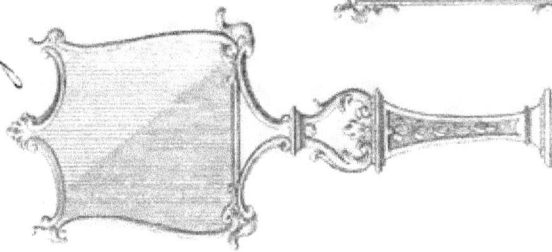

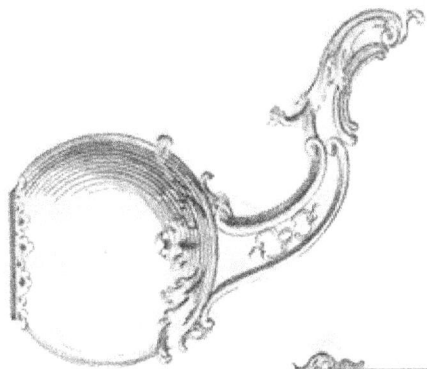

*L'anthorn.*

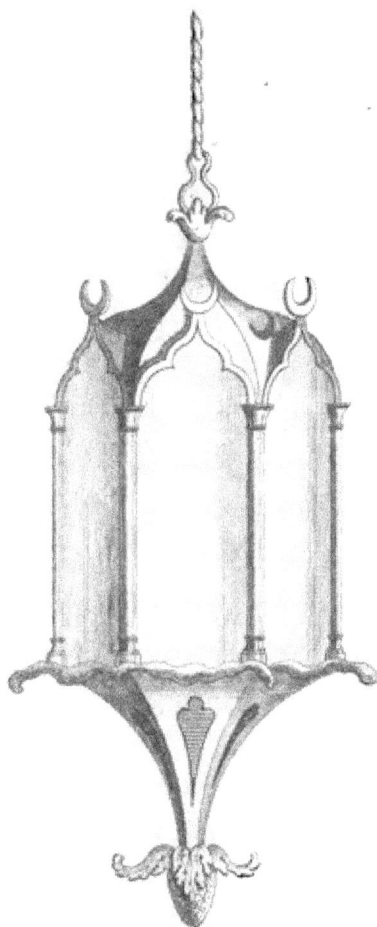

*Couse sculp.*

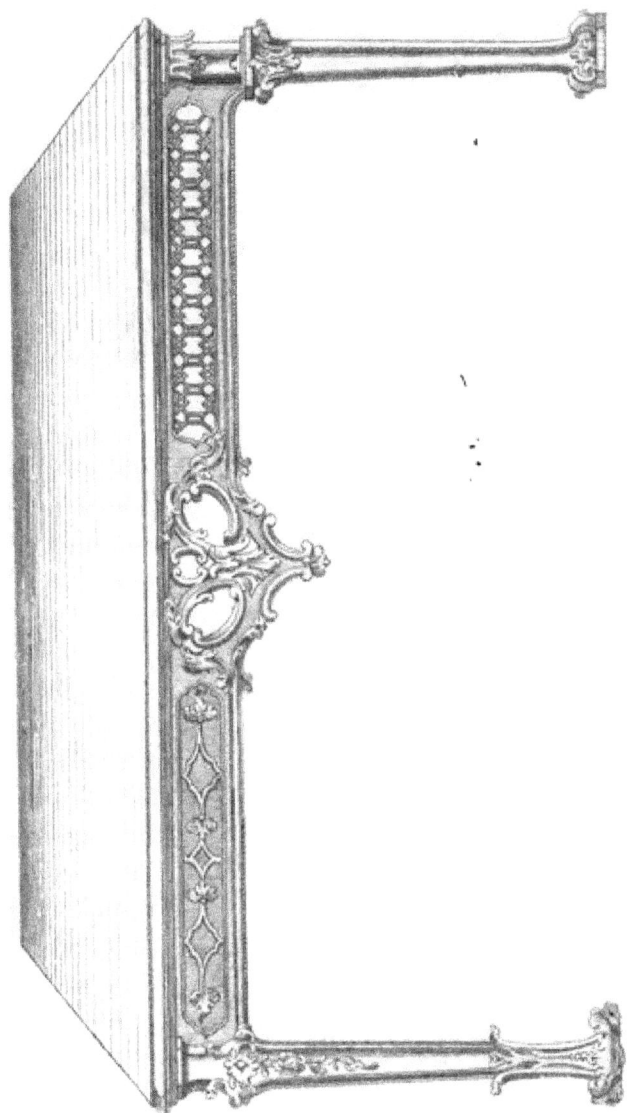

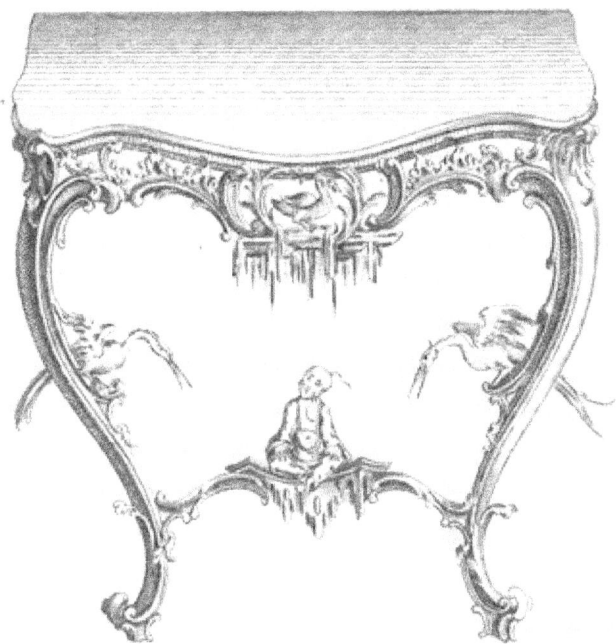

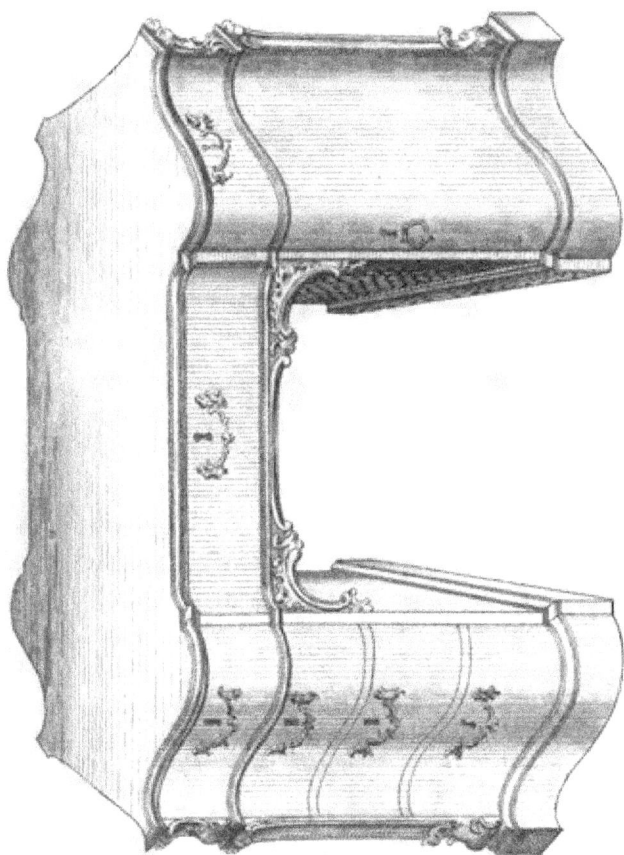

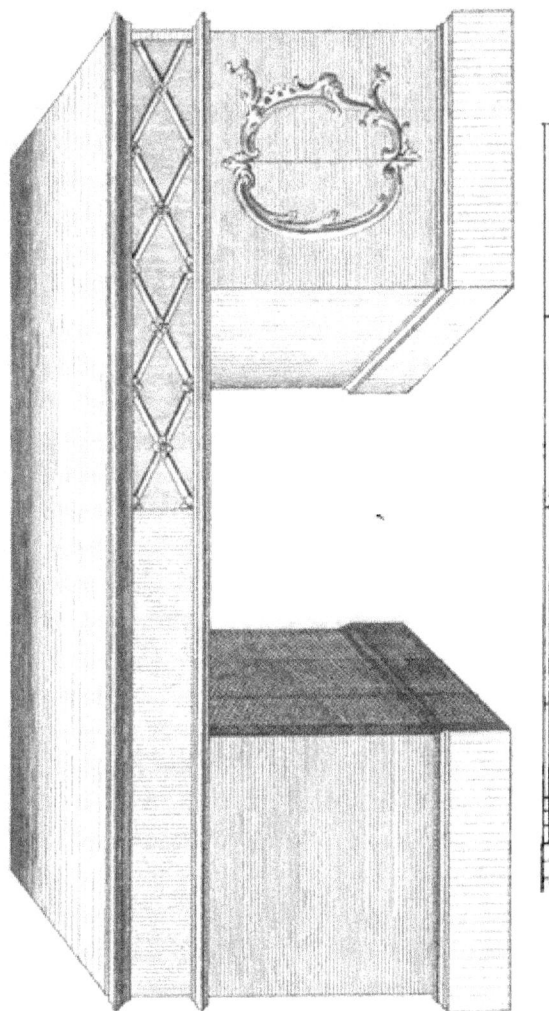

# Dressing Tables.

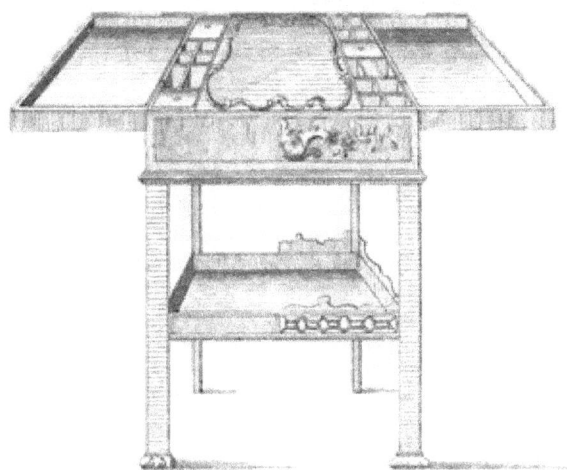

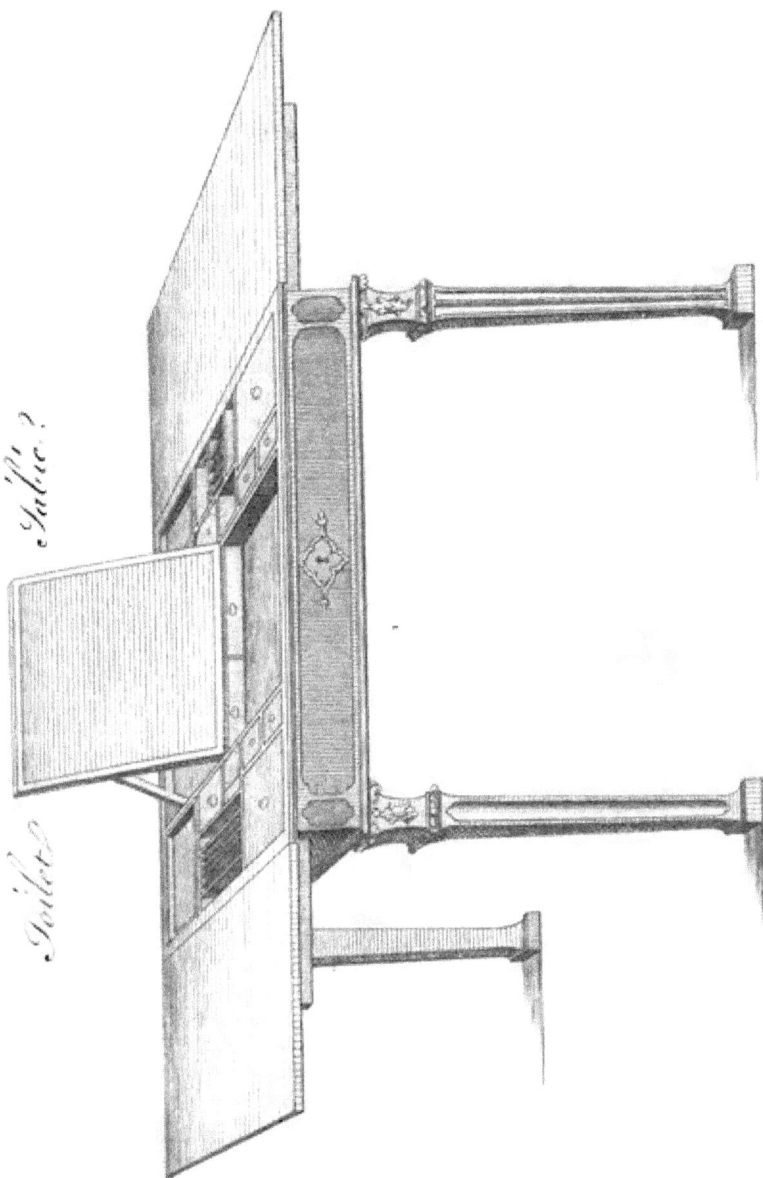

*Toilet.*

*Tab. V?*

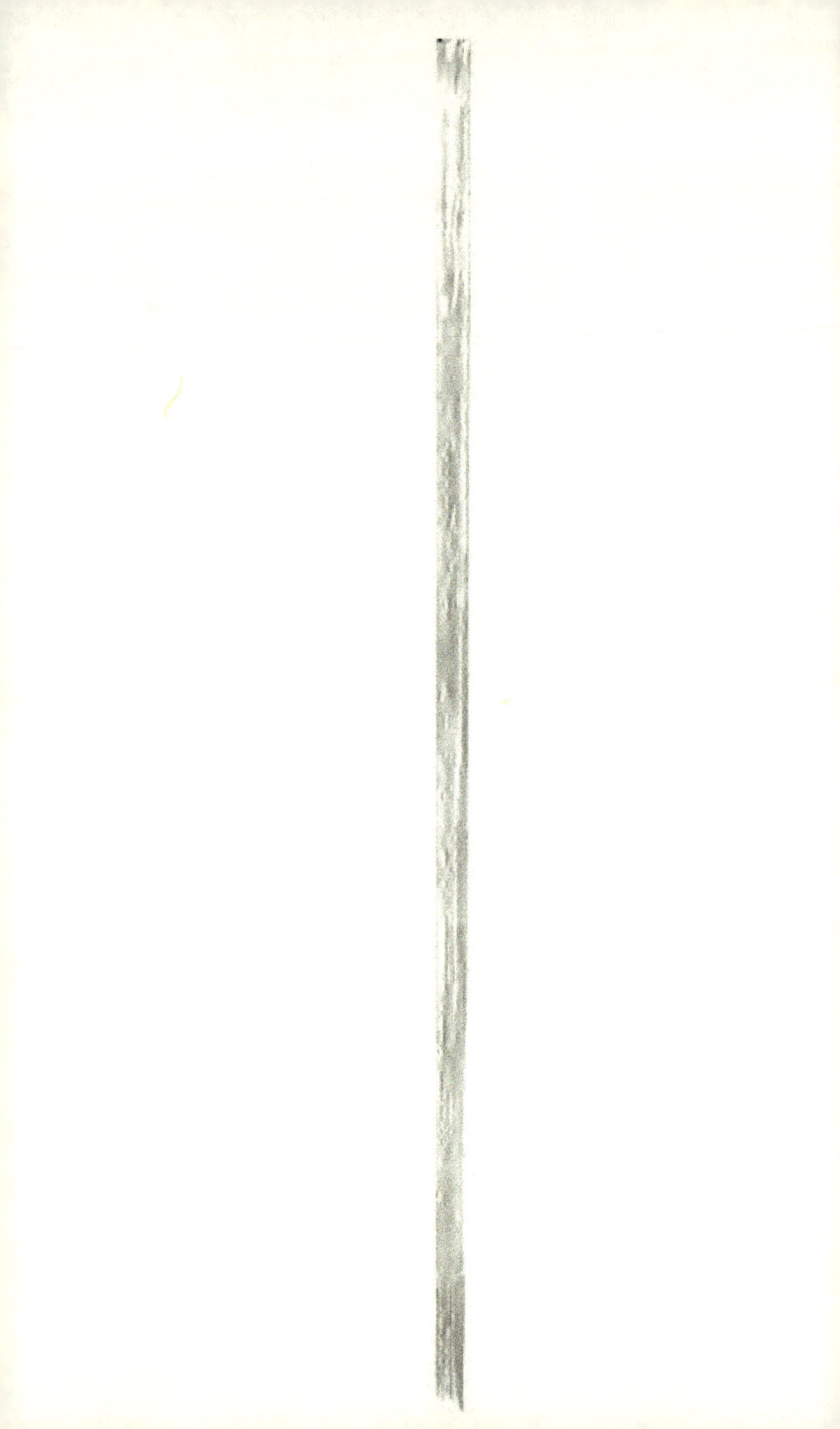

# Card Tables.

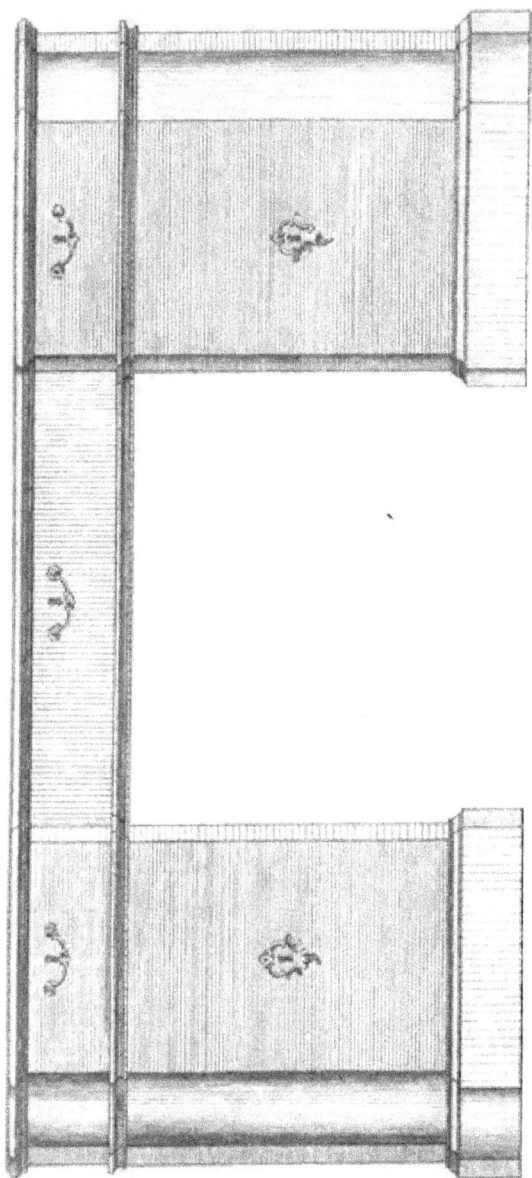

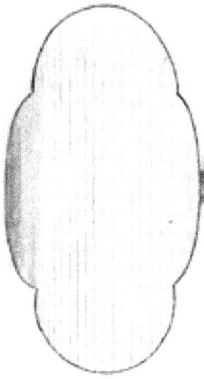

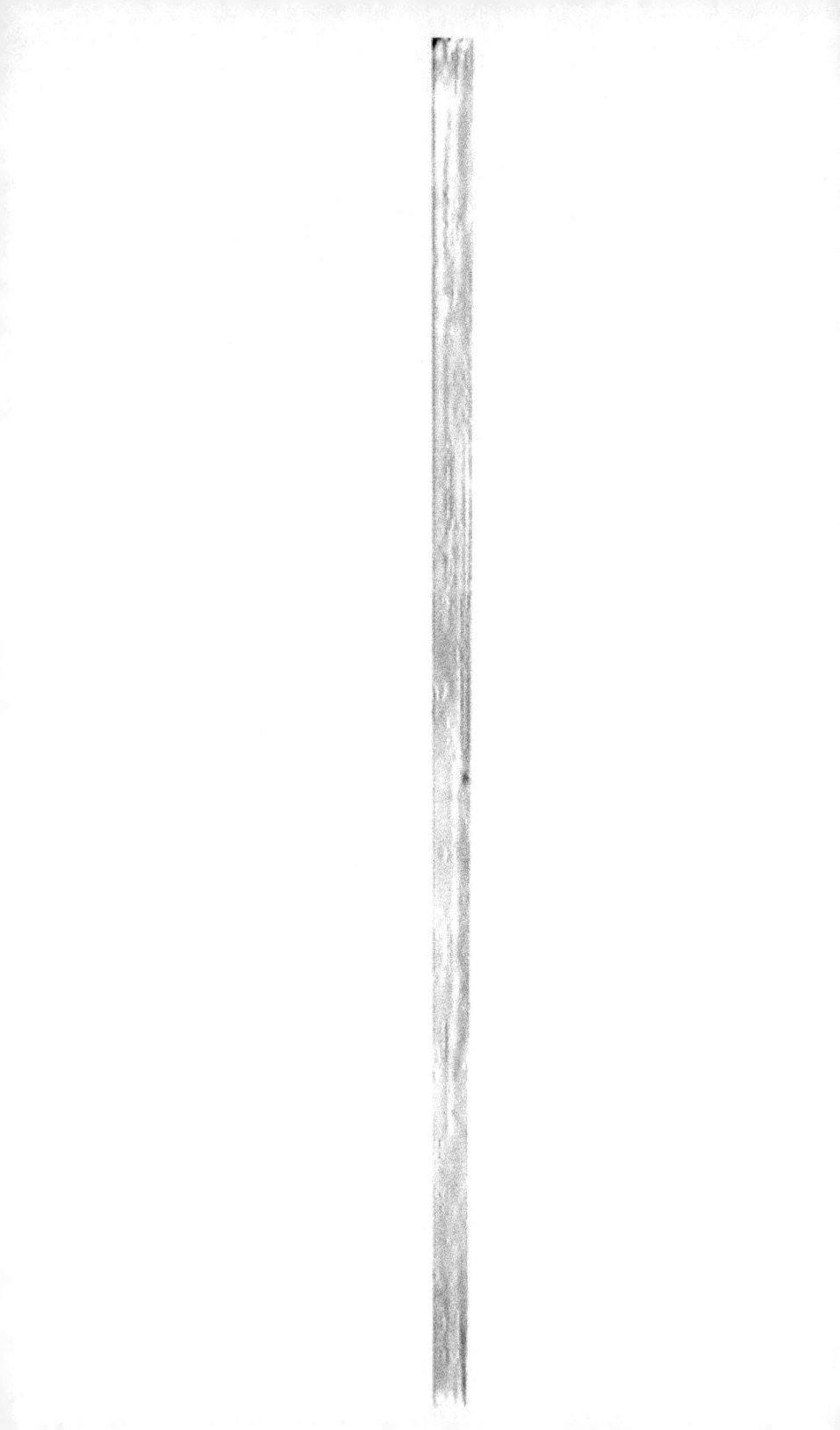

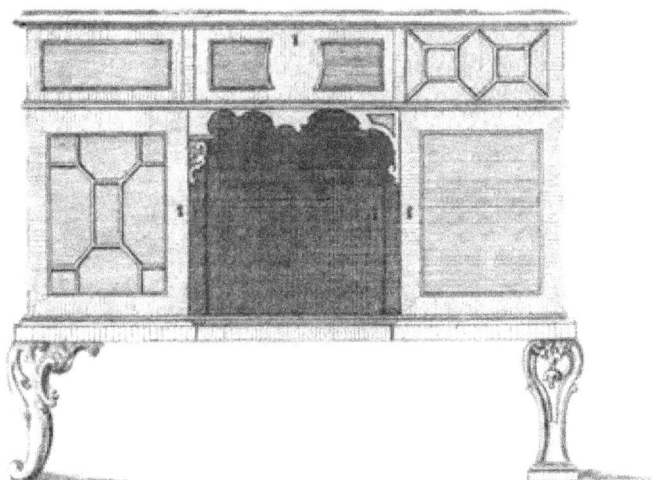

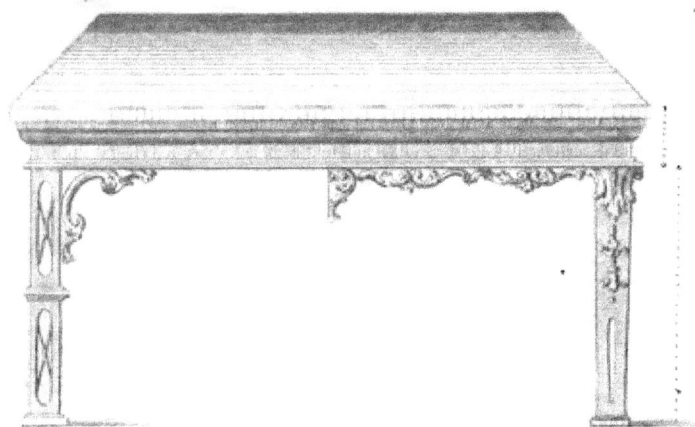

*Night Tables.*

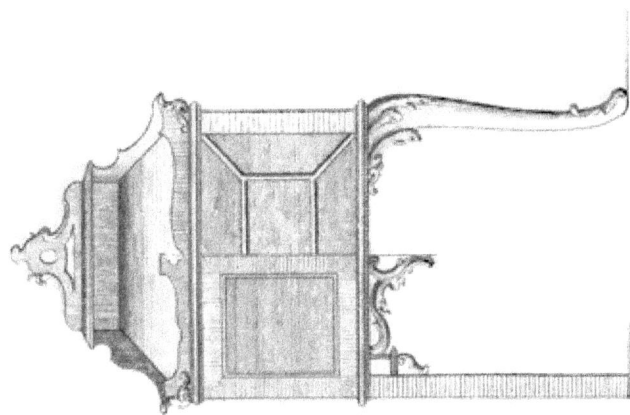

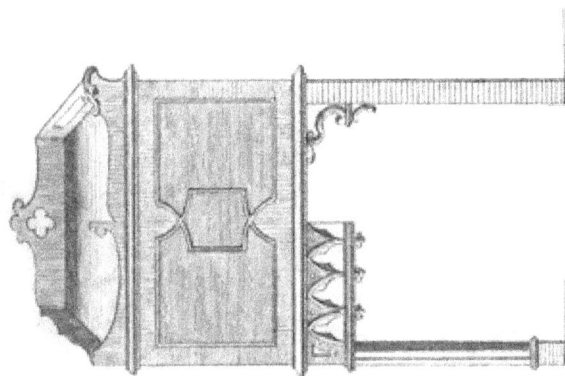

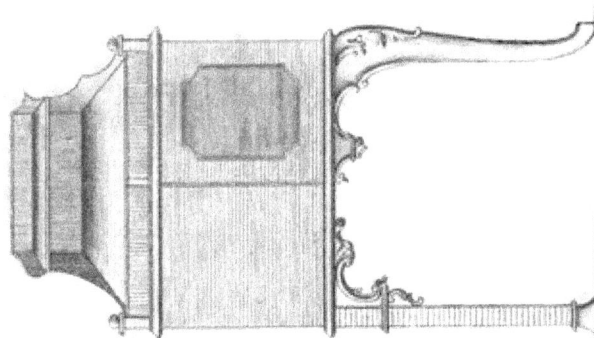

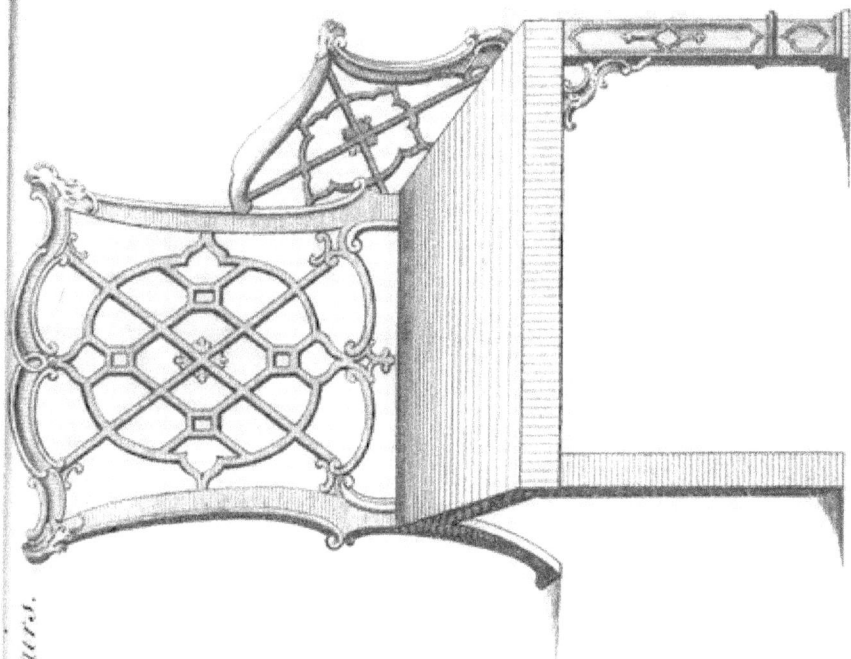

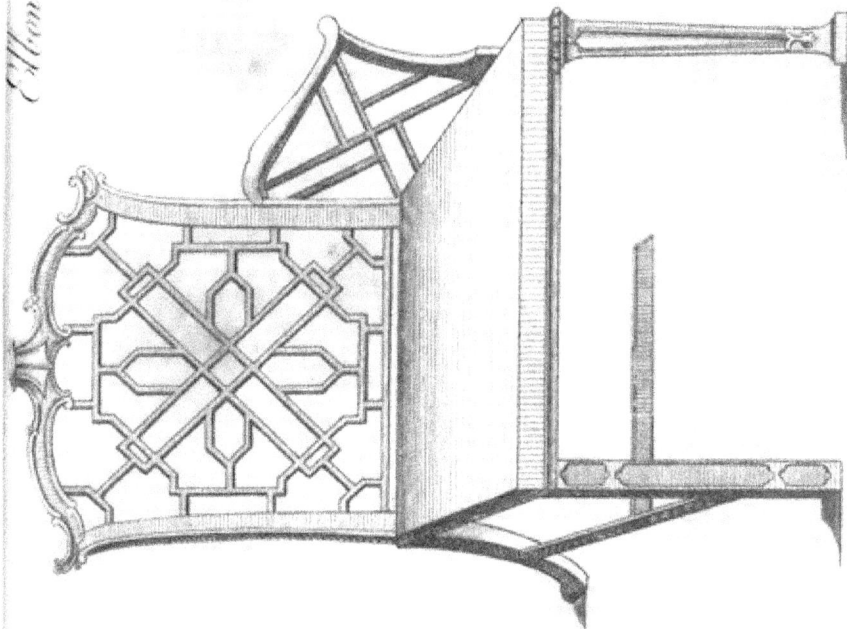

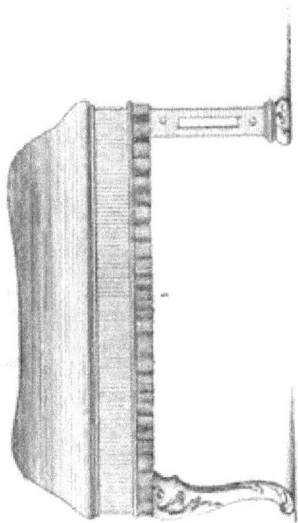

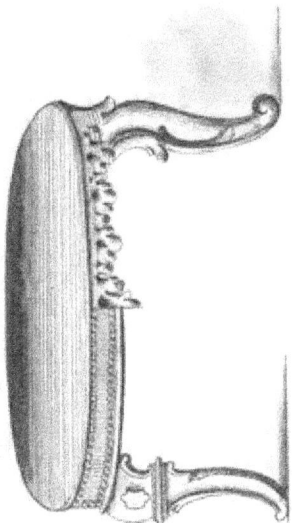

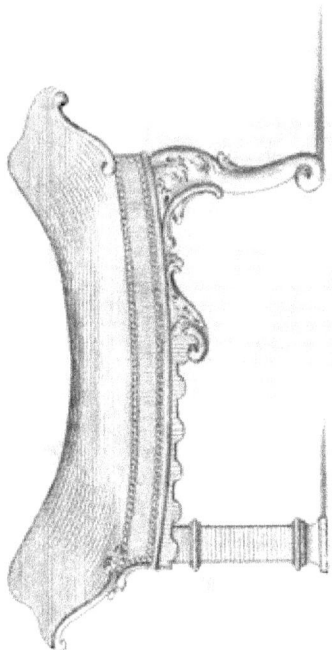

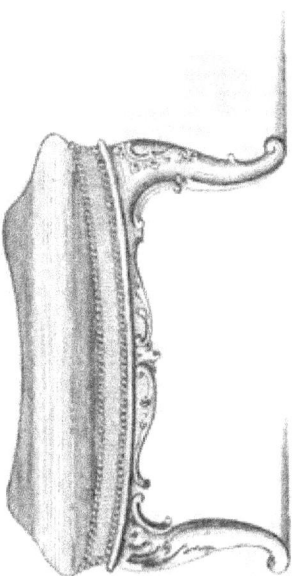

French Chairs.

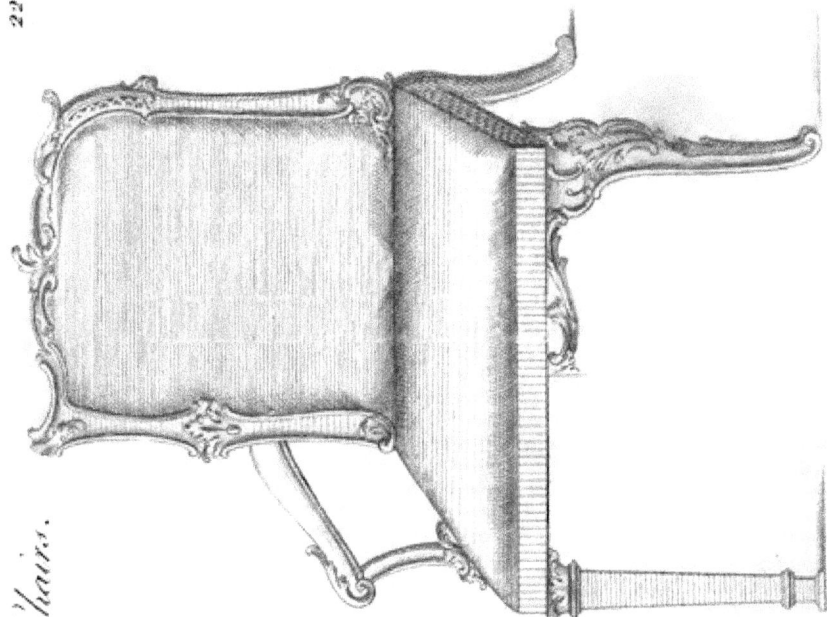

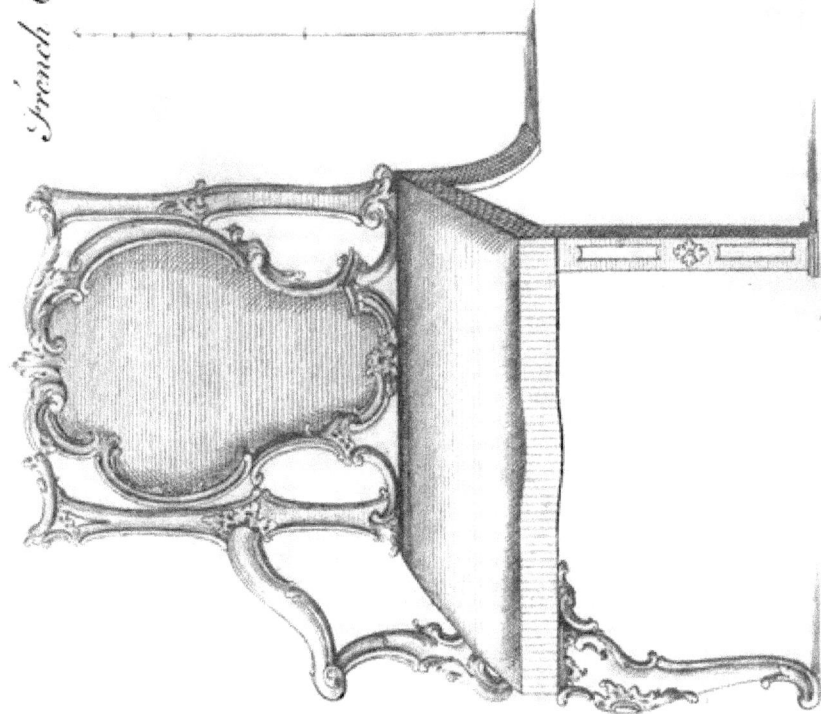

Chair with a Frett Bach.

*Gothic Chair.*

*Settee Couches.*

Corniches.

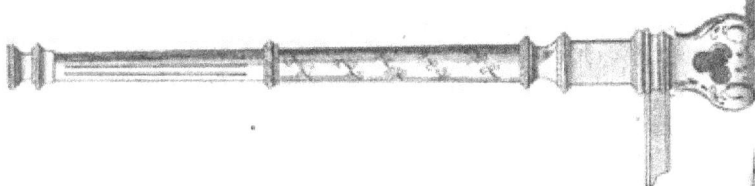

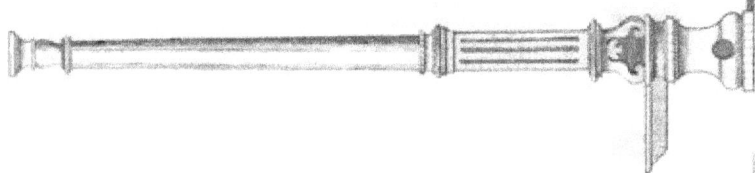

# *Bed*

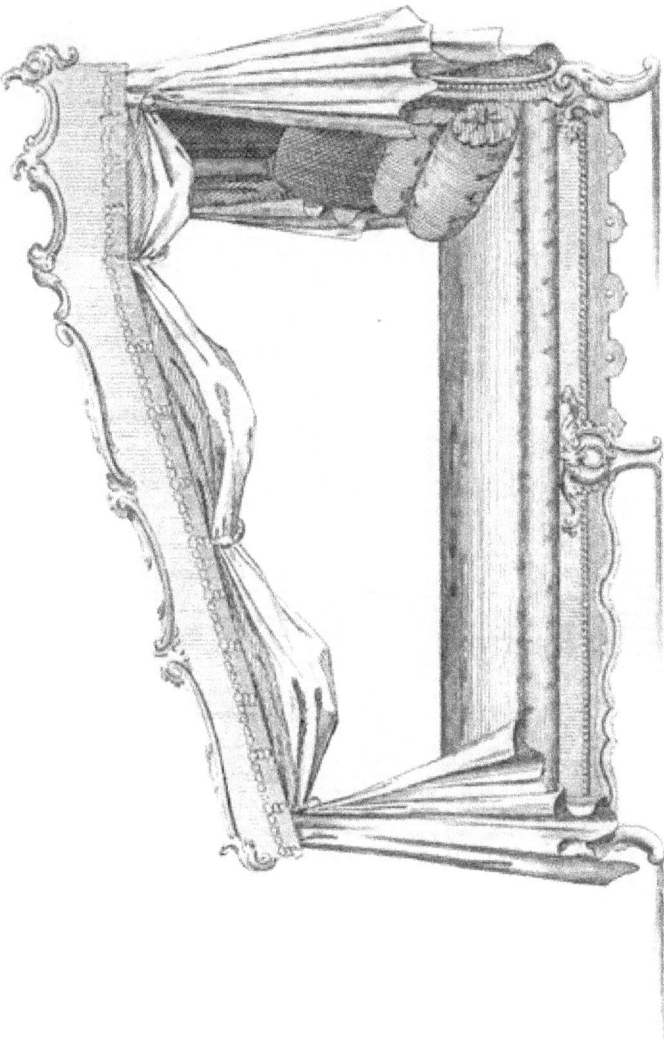

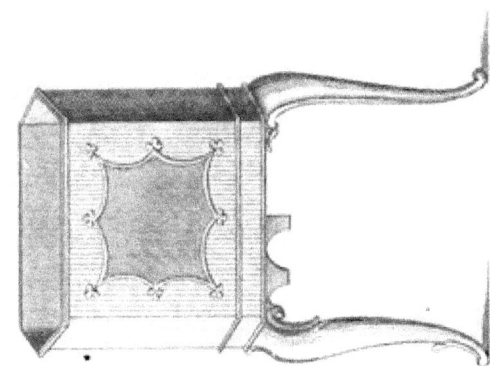

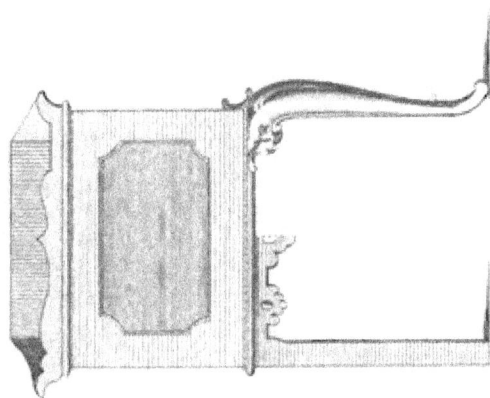

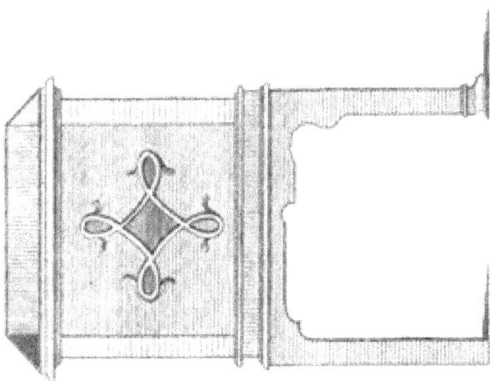

## 31

*Pedestals for Jars, Figures, &c.*

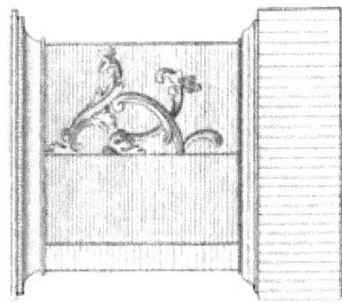

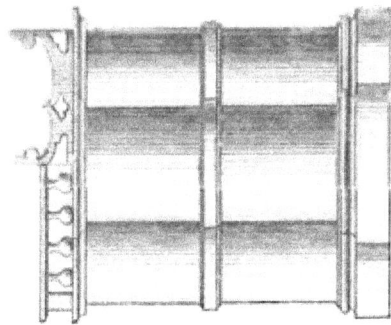
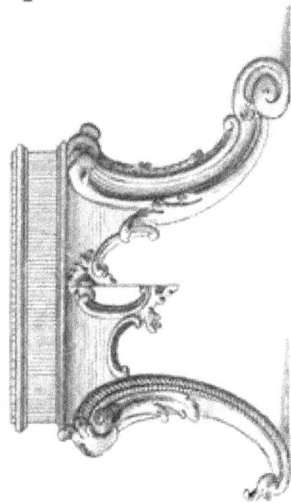

Cabinet.

# Cabinet with Shelves.

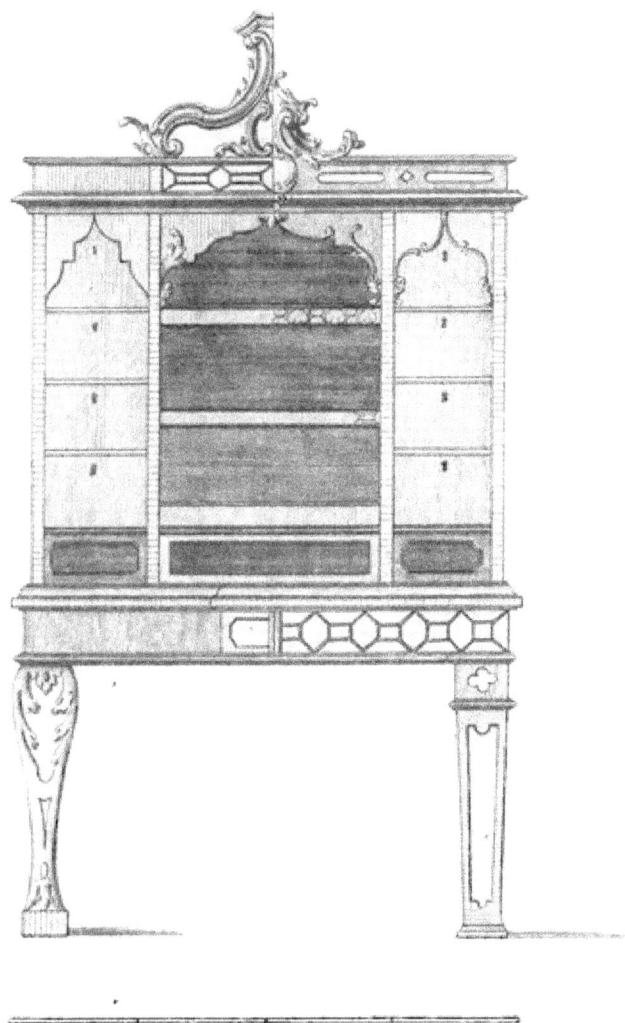

*Commode Cloaths Press.*

*Chests for Cloaths, &c.*

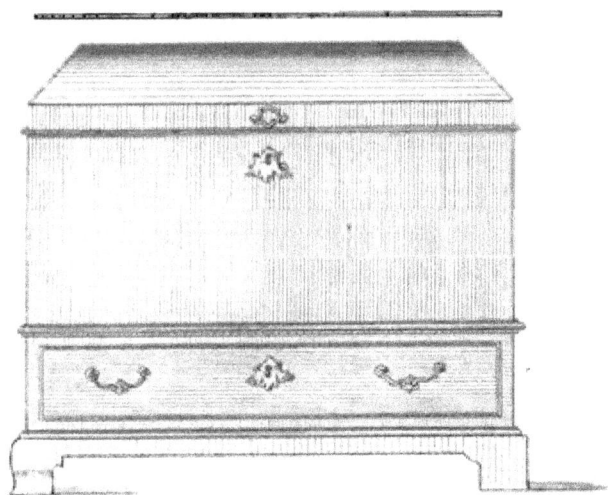

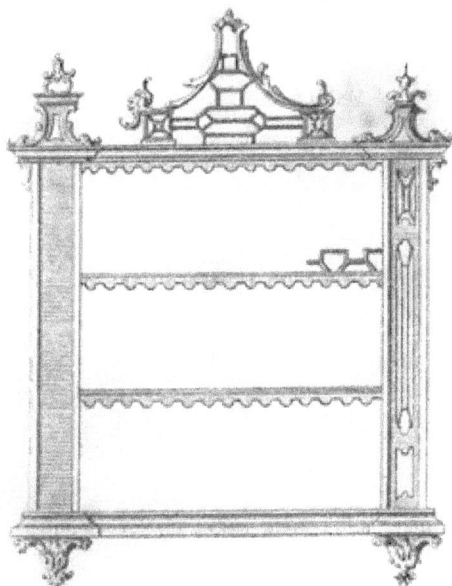

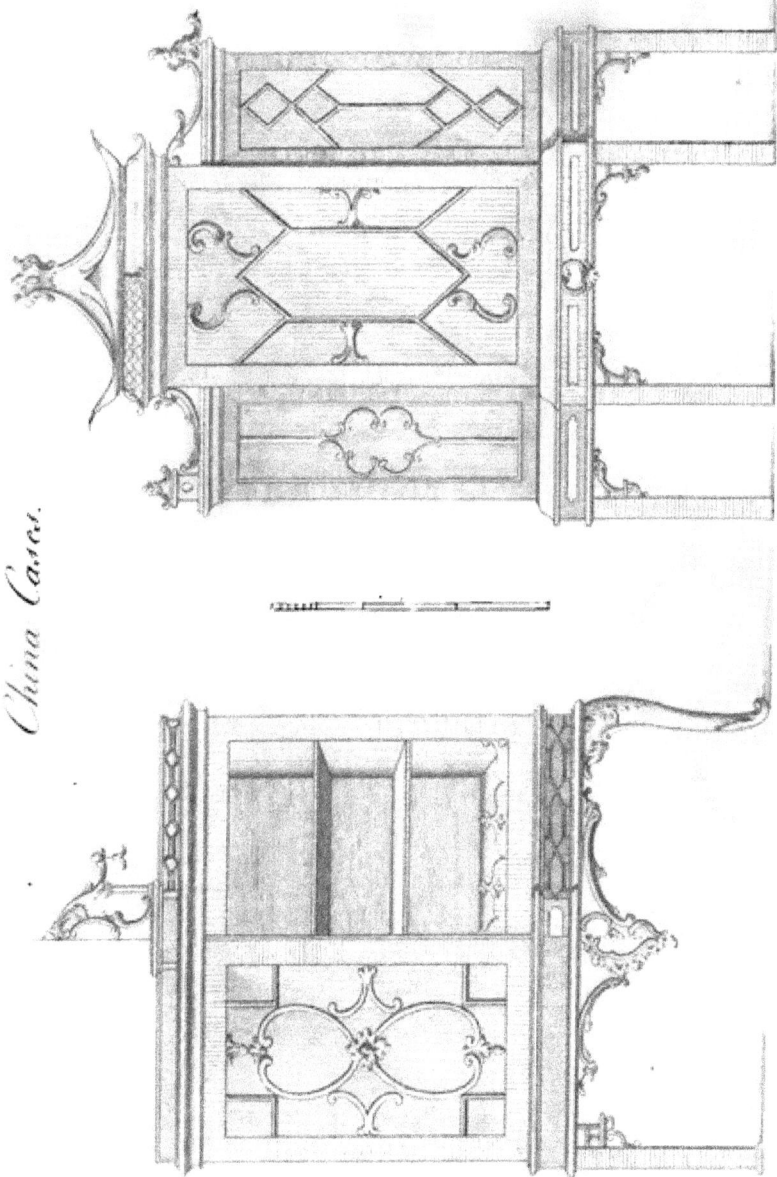

China Cases.

Trays.

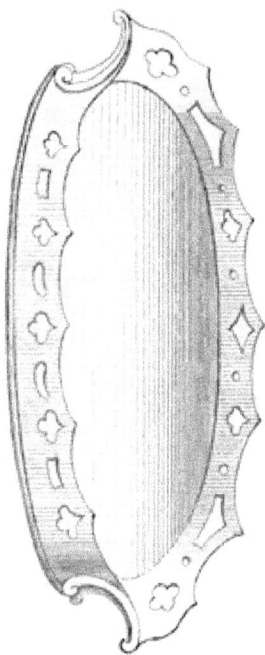

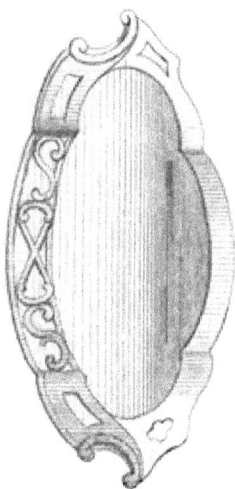

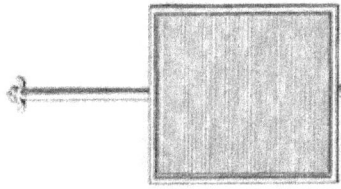

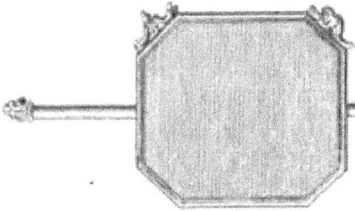

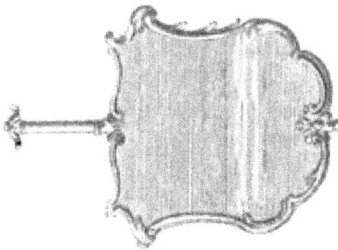

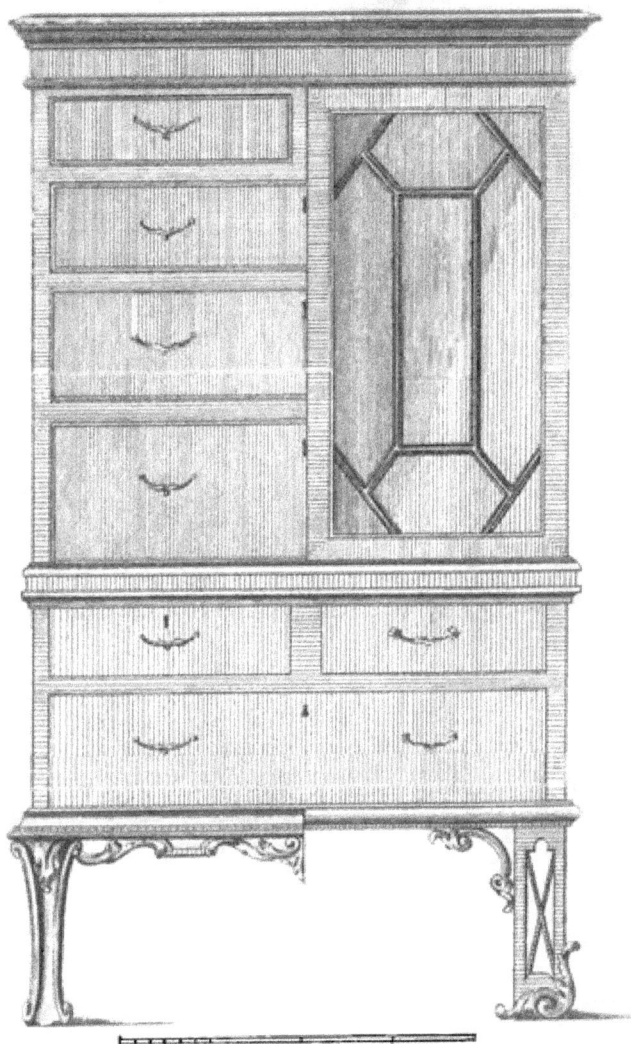

*Lady's Desk*

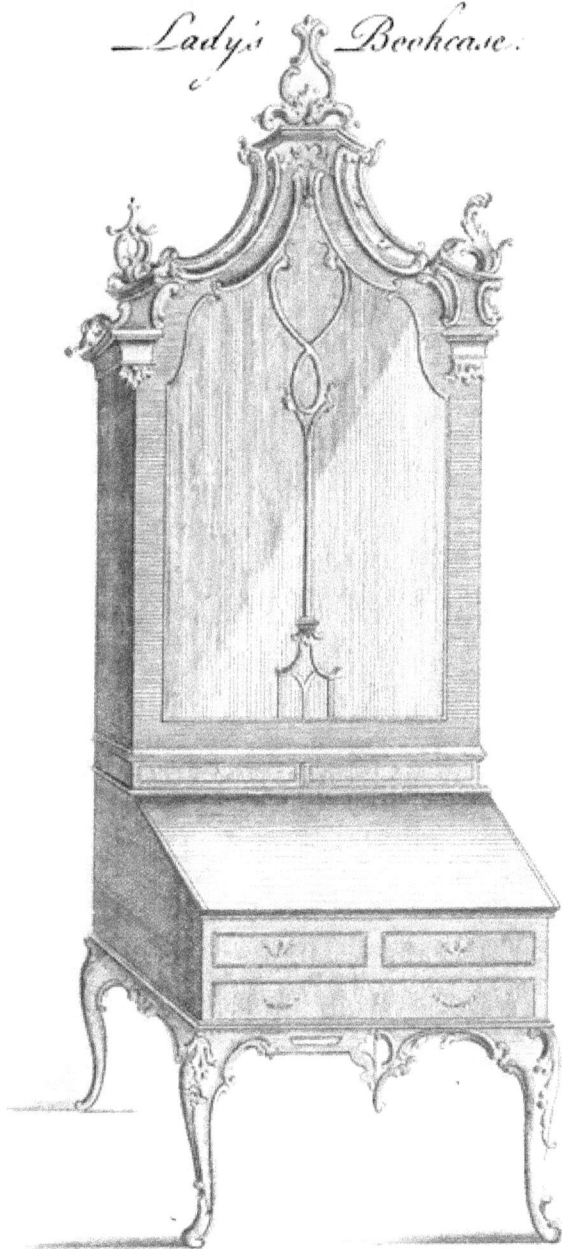

_Lady's Bookcase._

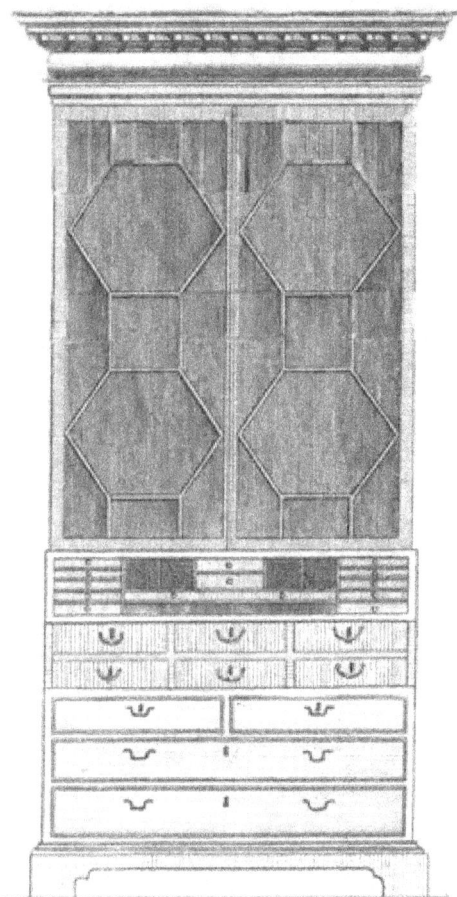

# Desk & Bookcase.

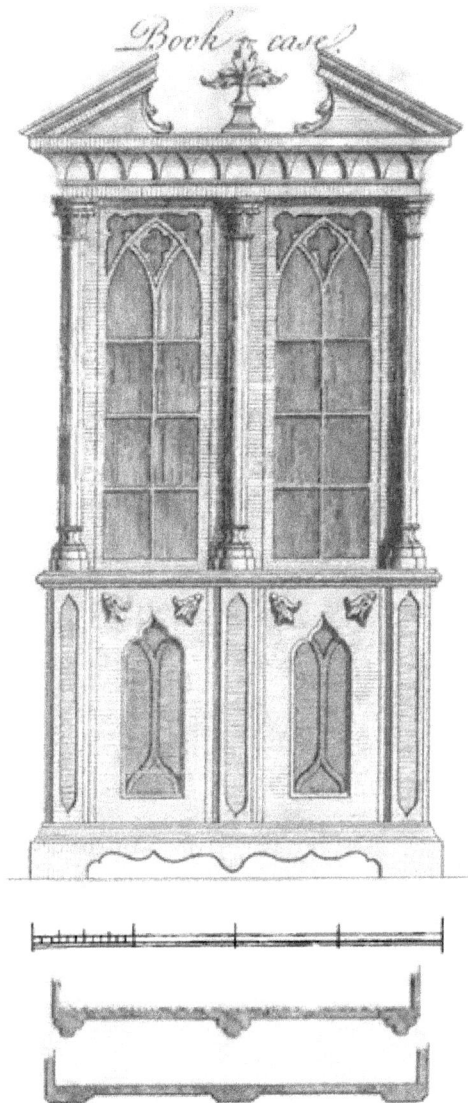

*Book-case.*

*Couse sculp.*

Gothic Door.

*Girondoles.*

# Chimney Glasses.

Chinese Sconce.

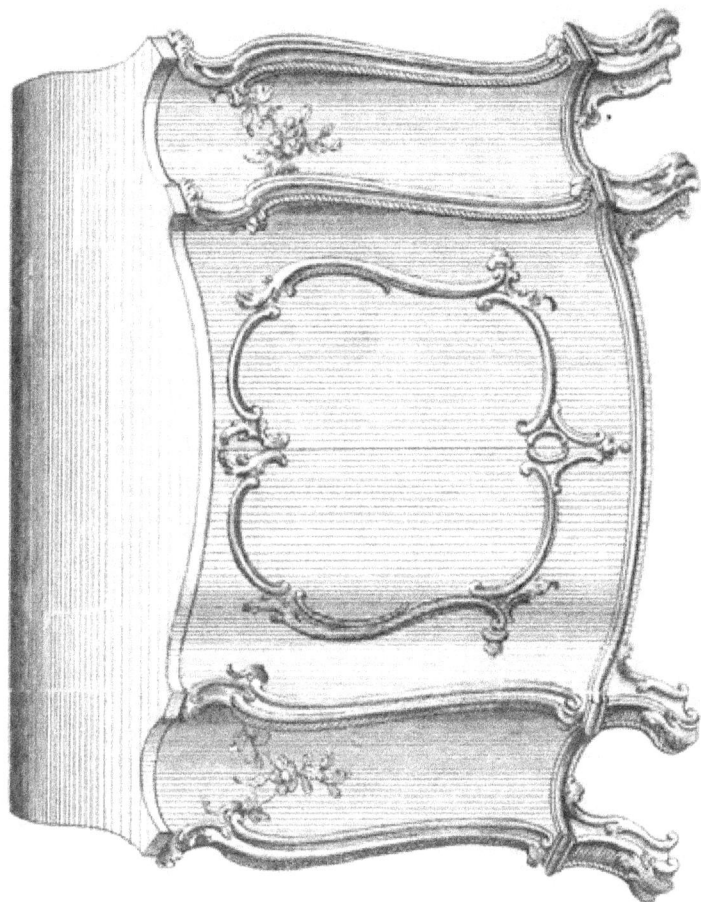